AF001222

Easy Christmas Melodies

with duet accompaniments

arranged by
Cynthia Pace

Contents

Jingle Bells 2

Deck the Halls 4

We Three Kings 6

Jolly Old Saint Nicholas 8

O Come Little Children 10

The First Noel 12

Joy to the World! 14

Up On the House-top 16

Silent Night 18

Angels We Have Heard On High 20

Go Tell It On The Mountain 22

We Wish You A Merry Christmas 24

Red-Toed Reindeer Blues 26

CHRISTMAS MELODIES CD recordings provide three "play-along" tracks for each duet as follows: 1) Melody and Accompaniment Parts together - performance tempo, 2) Melody and Accompaniment Parts together - practice tempo, 3) Accompaniment Part - performance tempo.

Lee Roberts Music Publications Inc.
Chatham, New York

DISTRIBUTED BY

HAL•LEONARD CORPORATION
7777 W. BLUEMOUND RD. P.O. BOX 13819 MILWAUKEE, WI 53212

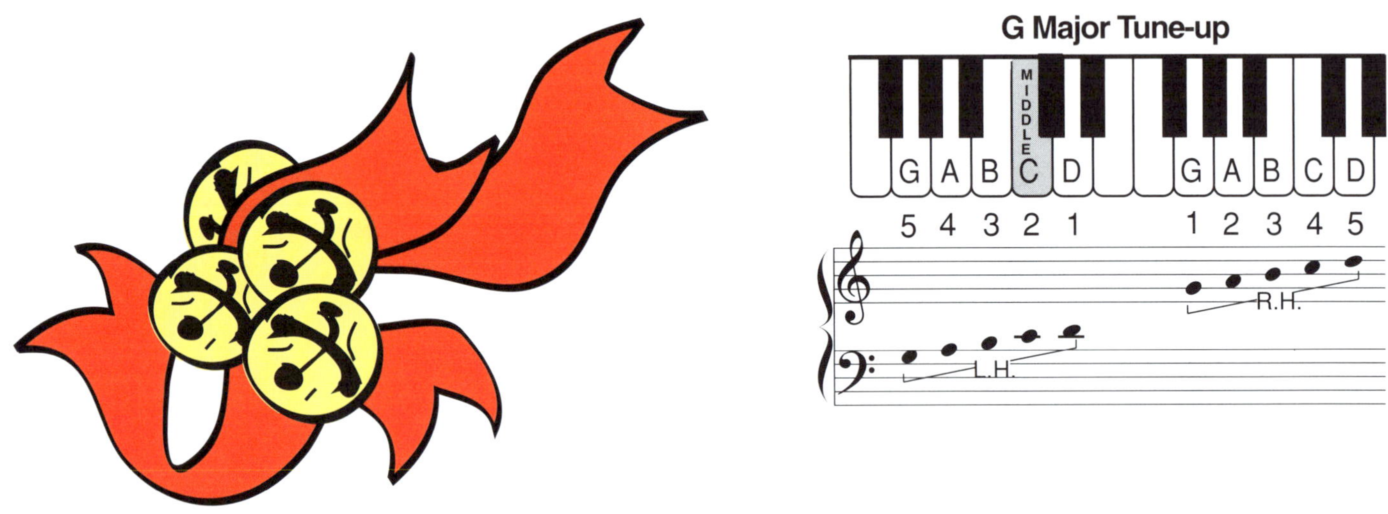

Accompaniment Part (Play solo part one octave higher than written):

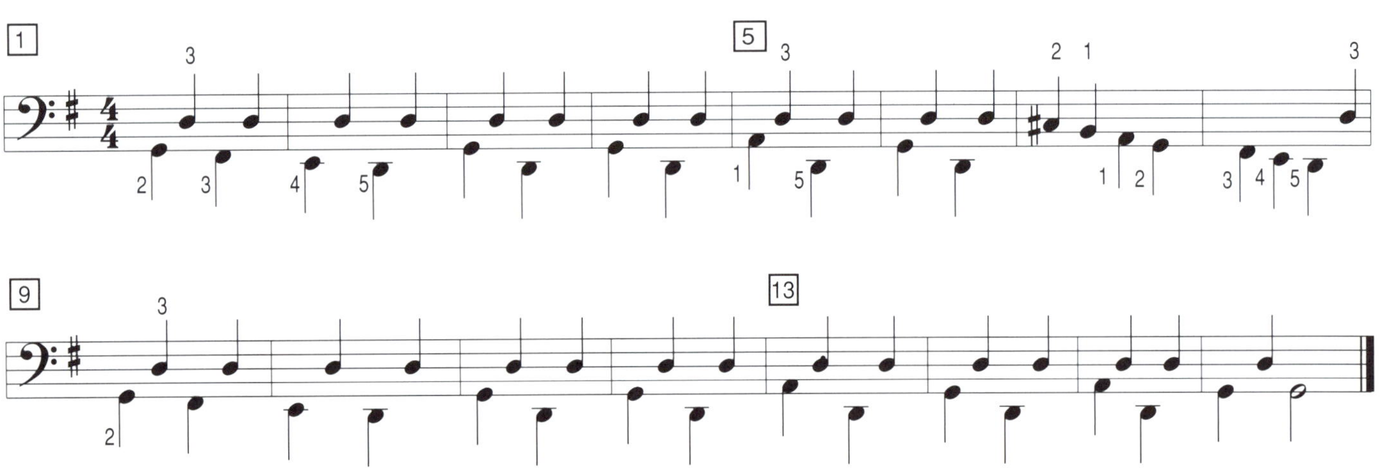

O, what fun it is to ride in a one-horse o-pen sleigh.___

Jin - gle bells, jin - gle bells, jin - gle all the way,

O, what fun it is to ride in a one-horse o-pen sleigh!

Deck the Halls

Welsh

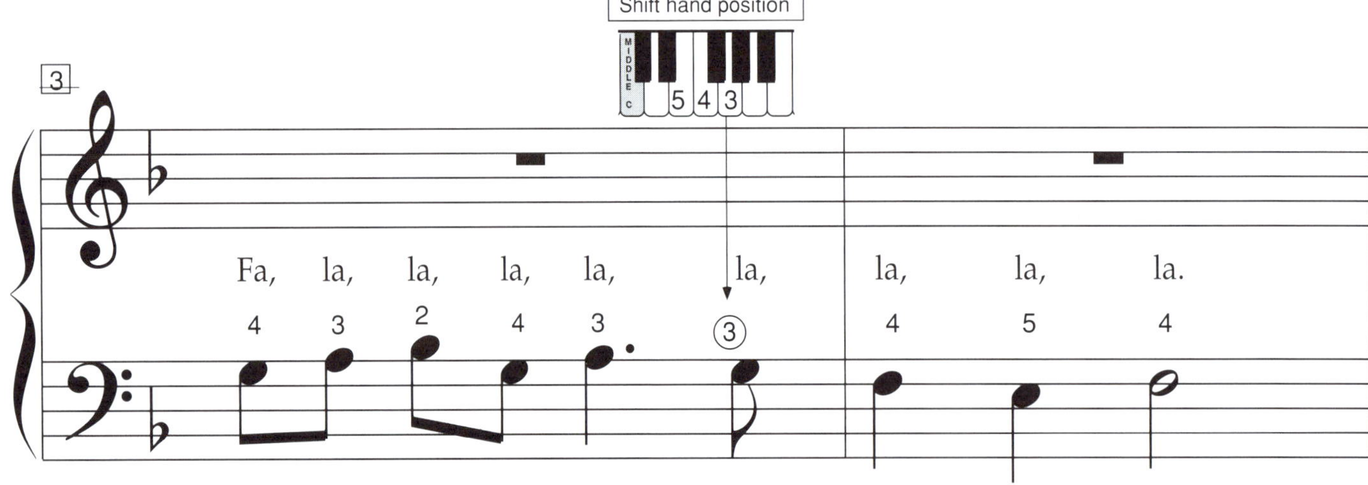

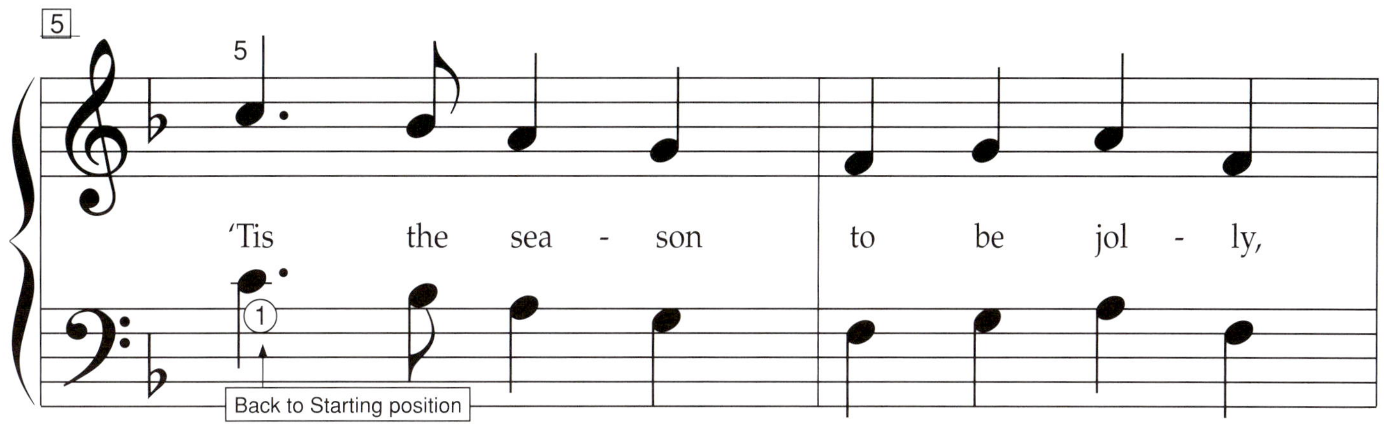

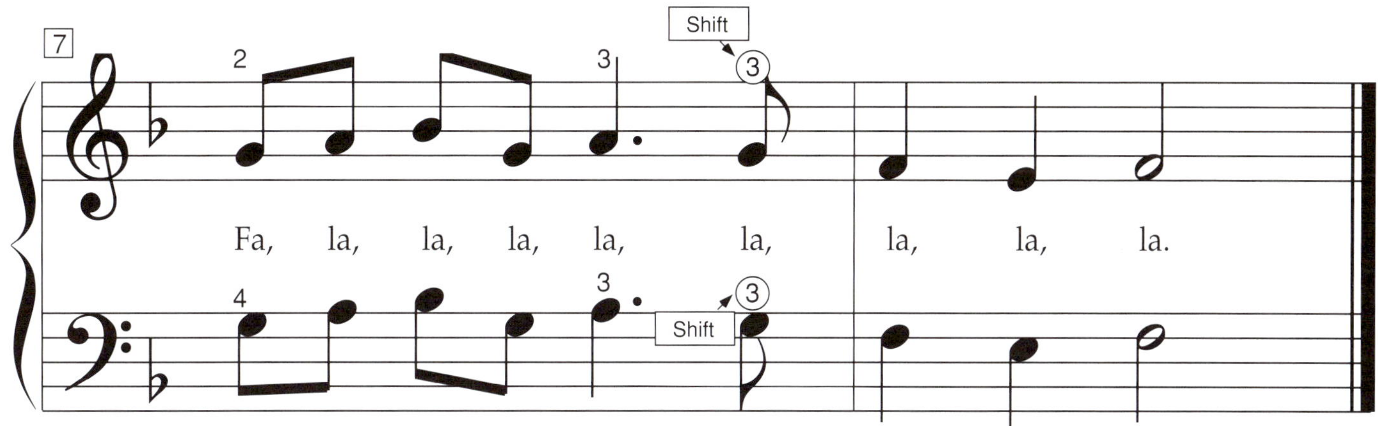

Accompaniment Part (Play solo part one octave higher than written):

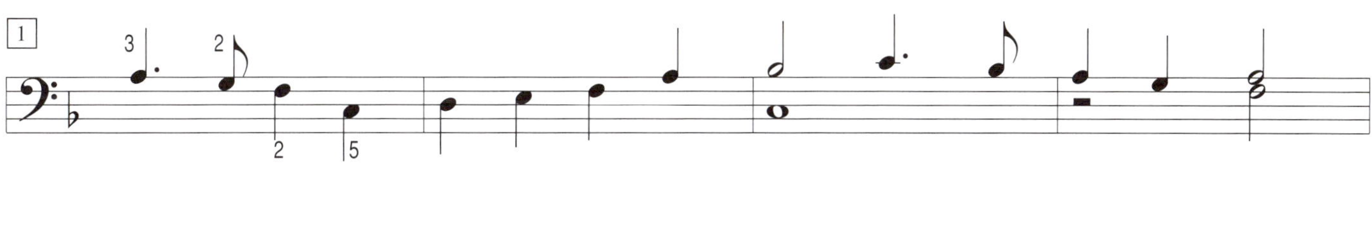

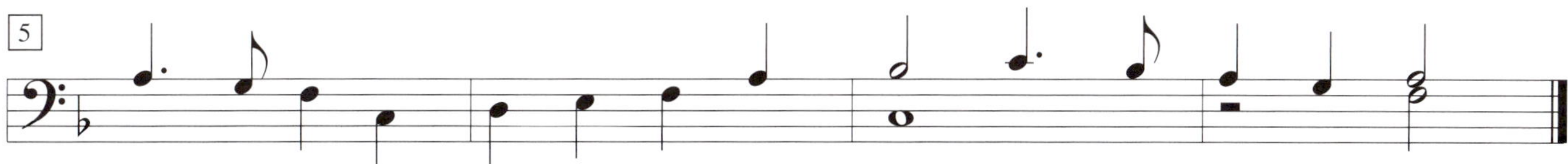

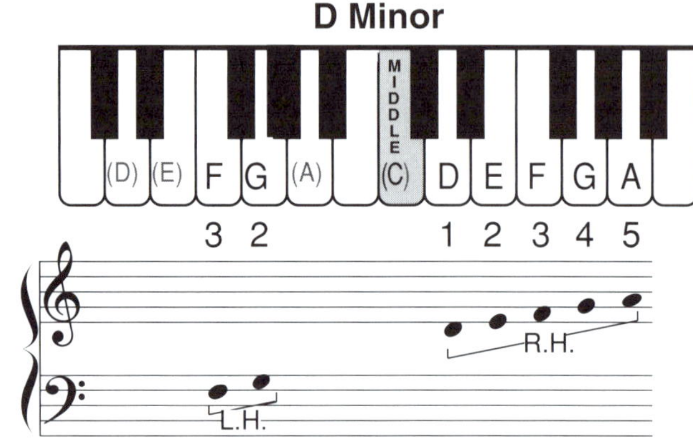

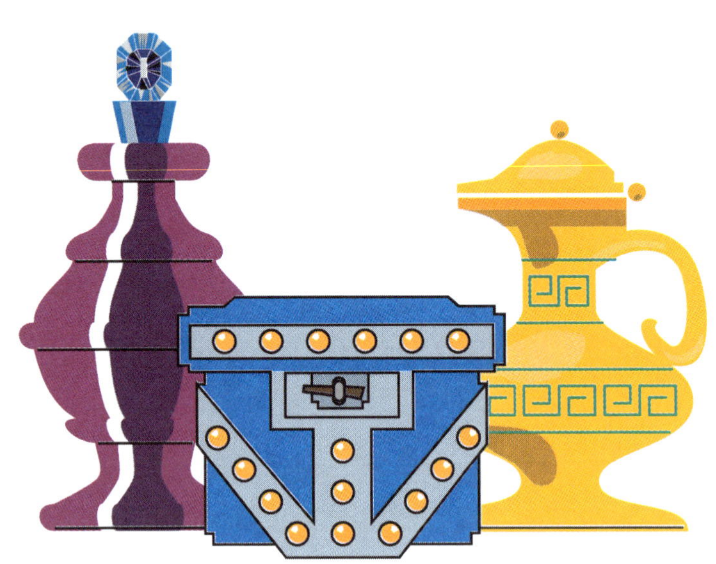

We Three Kings

John H. Hopkins

*D minor and F major are RELATIVE KEYS. They share the same key signature.

Accompaniment Part (Play solo part one octave higher than written):

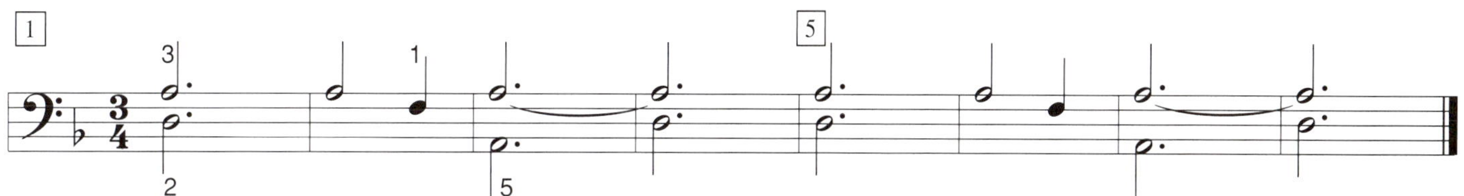

Jolly Old Saint Nicholas

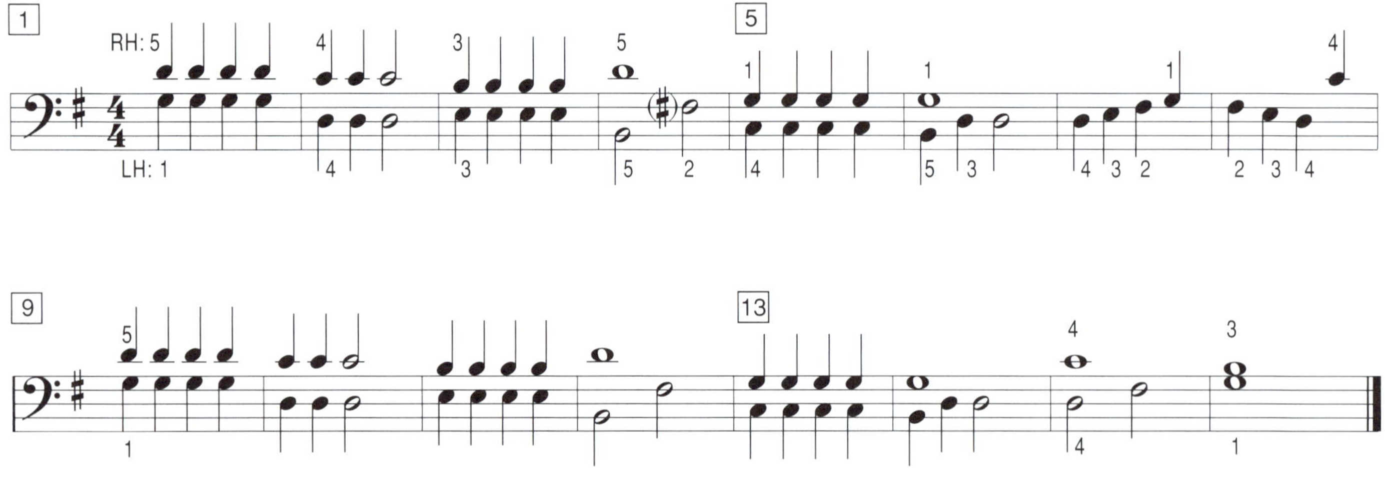

Don't you tell a sin - gle soul what I'm going to say;

Christ-mas Eve is com-ing soon, now you dear old man,

Whis-per what you'll bring to me, tell me if you can.

to Santa Claus

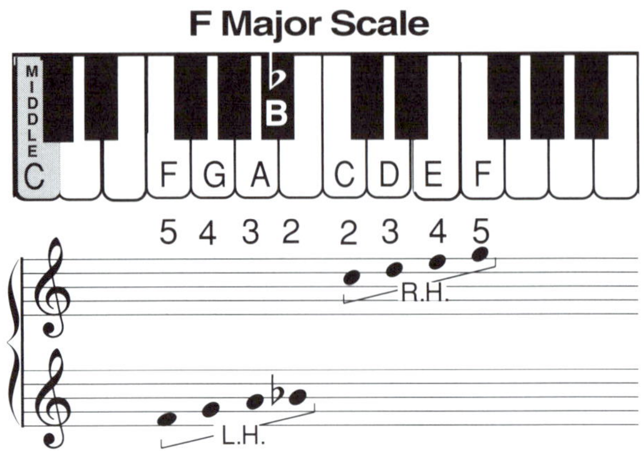

O Come Little Children

J.A.P. Schulz

Accompaniment Part (Play solo part as written):

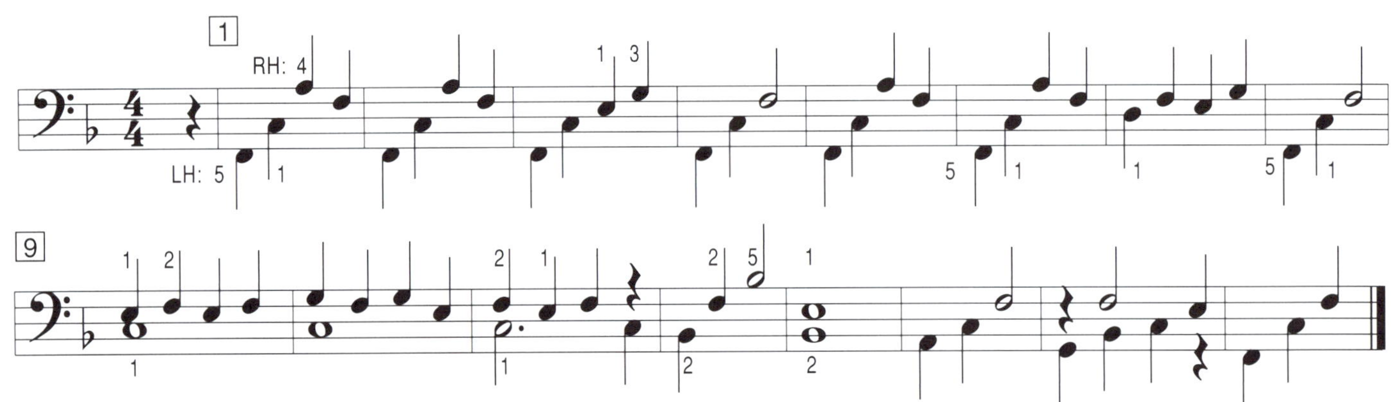

lies the sweet in- fant so ten - der and small. Now
"Glo - ry to God!" sing the an - gels on high, Then
"peace up - on earth!" heaven-ly voi - ces re - ply.

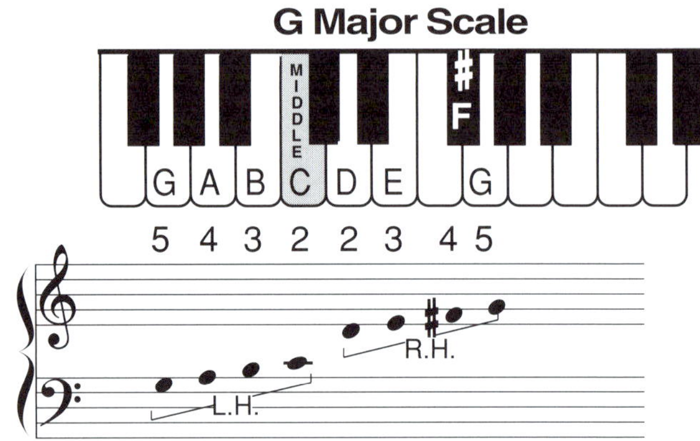

The First Noel

<u>Accompaniment Part</u> (Play solo part one octave higher than written):

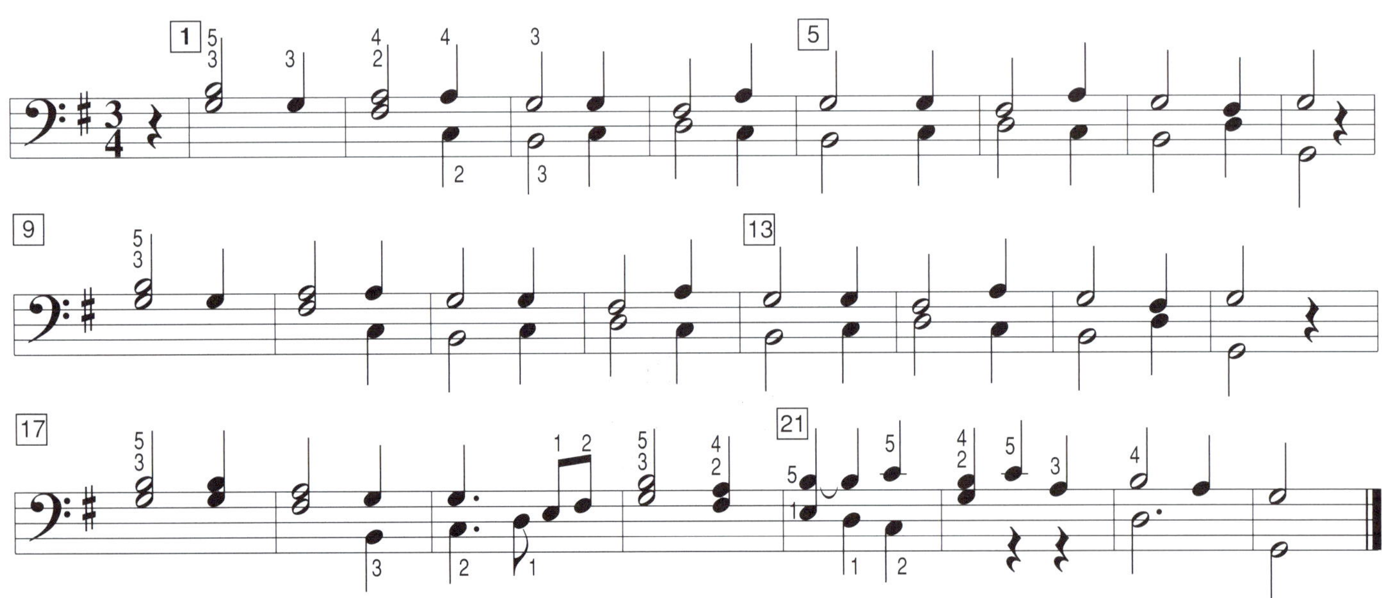

cer - tain poor shep - herds in fields as they lay, In___
fields___ where they lay__ Keep - ing their sheep, On a
cold win - ter's night __ that was___ so deep. No -
el,___ No - el, No - el, No - el,
Born is the King___ of Is - ra - el.

Accompaniment Part (Play solo part as written):

earth re - ceive her King;___ Let ev -__ 'ry__
heart____ pre - pare__ Him__ room,___ And
heav'n and na - ture__ sing, And__ heav'n and na - ture__ sing, And
heav'n__ And heav'n__ and na - ture sing.
2424

Up On the House-top

B. R. Hanby

<u>Accompaniment Part</u> (Play solo part one octave higher than written):

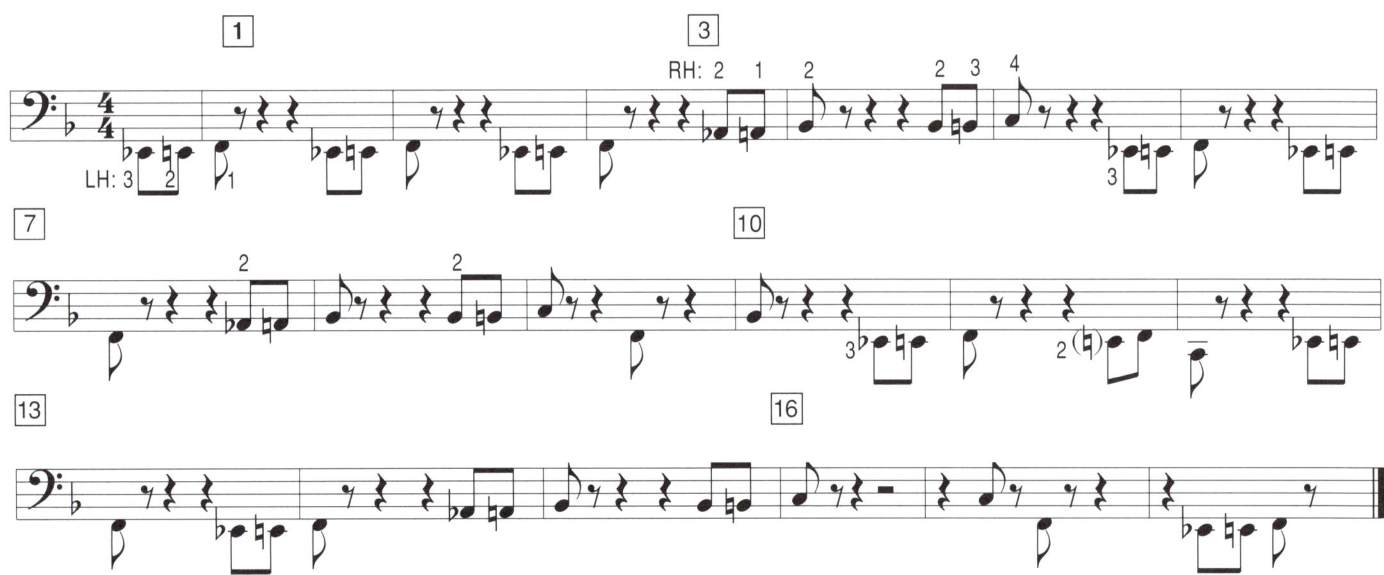

San - ta Claus; Down through the chim - ny with lots of toys,

All for the lit - tle ones, Christ-mas joys. Ho, ho, ho, Who would-n't go!

Ho, ho, ho, Who would-n't go!____ Up on the house - top

click, click, click, Down through the chim - ney with good Saint Nick!

C Major Scale Tones

Silent Night

Franz Gruber
Joseph Mohr

Key of C Major

Accompaniment Part (Play solo part one octave higher than written):

6
calm, All is bright. 'Round yon vir - gin
11
Moth - er and Child. Ho - ly In - fant so ten - der and
16
Shift Right Hand position
MIDDLE C
mild, Sleep in heav - en -ly peace,
21
Sleep___ in heav - en -ly peace.

Angels We Have Heard On High

Key of F Major

French

Accompaniment Part (Play solo part one octave higher than written):

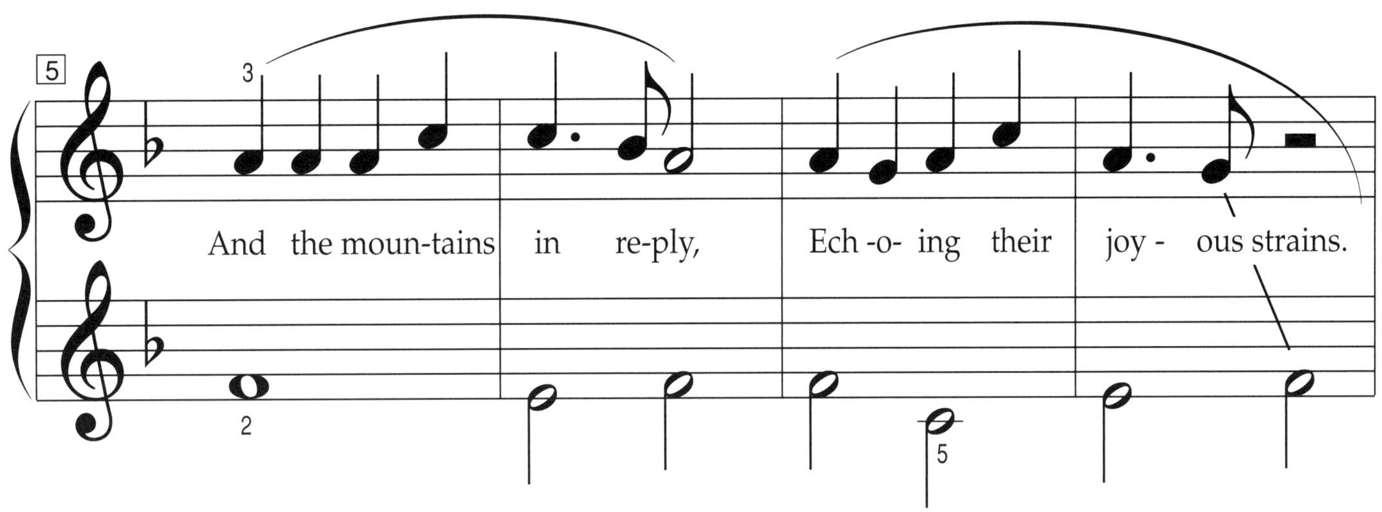
5
3
And the moun-tains in re-ply, Ech-o-ing their joy - ous strains.
2

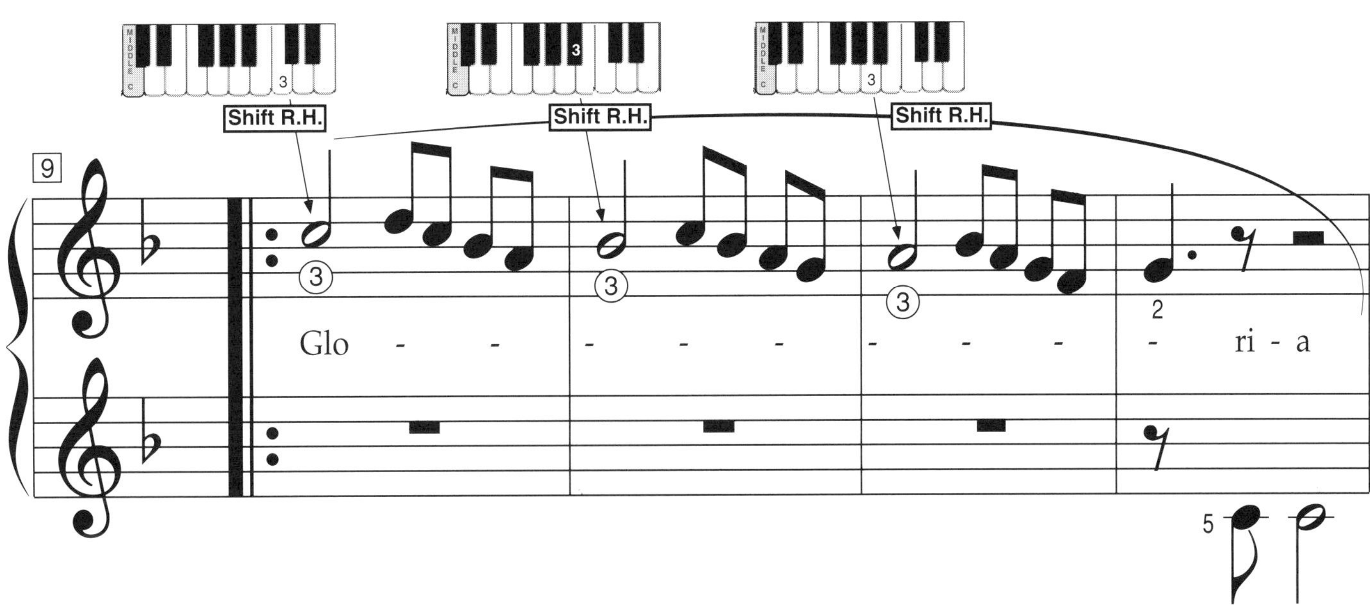
MIDDLE C   3   Shift R.H.
MIDDLE C   3   Shift R.H.
MIDDLE C   3   Shift R.H.
9
3   3   3   2
Glo - - - - - - - - ri - a
5

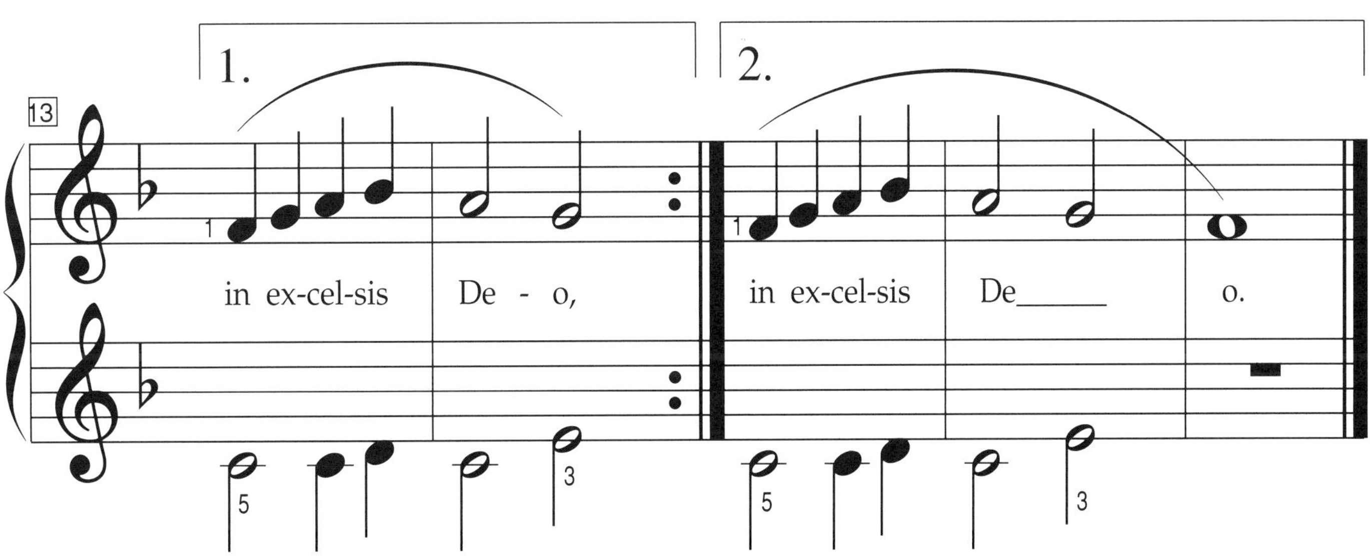
1.   2.
13
1   1
in ex-cel-sis De - o,   in ex-cel-sis De_____ o.
5   3   5   3

Go Tell It On The Mountain

Spiritual

<u>Accompaniment Part</u> (Play solo part one octave higher than written):

o - ver the hills and ev - 'ry where;___ Go tell it on the

moun - tain That Je - sus Christ is born!_______

We Wish You A Merry Christmas

Accompaniment Part (Play solo part one octave higher than written):

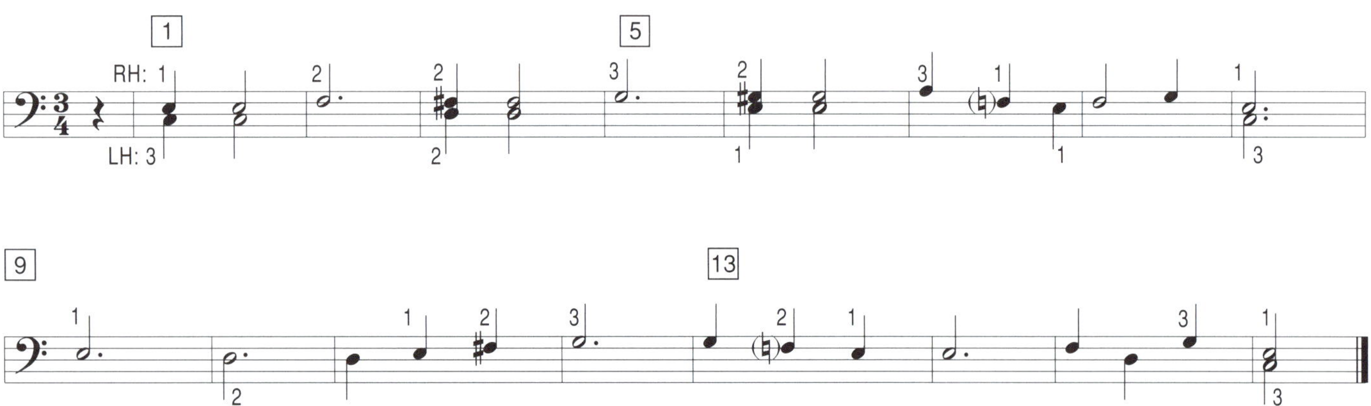

5
3
2
wish you a Mer-ry   Christ-mas,   and a   hap - py New   Year.
2
2

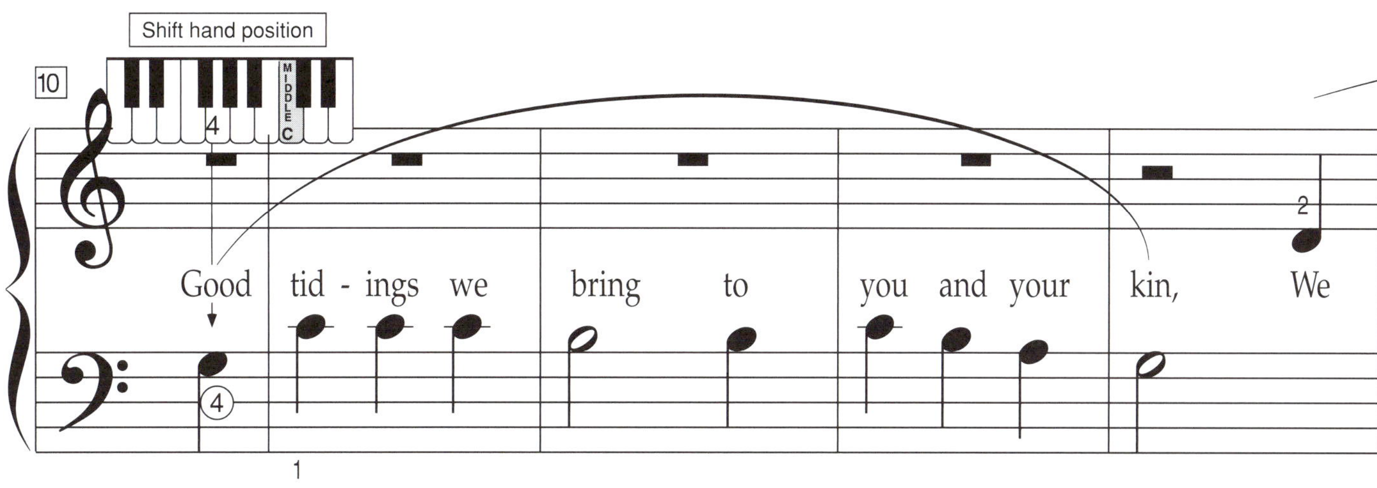
Shift hand position
MIDDLE C
10
4
4
1
2
Good   tid - ings we   bring   to   you   and your   kin,   We

13
3
5
2
1
wish   you a Mer-ry   Christ-mas and a   hap - py New   Year!
1
2
Back to Starting position
3

Jazzy and Rhythmically Free

Red-Toed Reindeer Blues

Cynthia Pace
words/music

F Blues

Accompaniment Part (Play accompaniment 1 octave LOWER. Play solo part as written):

3
5 4 3 2 1
feet glowed silver -y
save the day to -
join you with de -
red, but all his
night.___ We're o - ver
friends they
load - ed, we'll be too
(3rd Verse: Skip from here to Coda, pg. 28.
6
3 4 5 1 2
teased him, so
slow to go, with-
sad - ly this he
out your fleet - foot
said: "I've got the
flight! O red - toed
rein - deer
Twin - kle
10
1 2
blues, those bad old
deer, for you we'll
rein - deer
clap and
blues, blue red -toed
cheer, with your red
rein - deer
toes so
14
4 1
blues." Then
spry, our
San - ta called out nod-din' his
trip will sure - ly be out of
head:
sight!"

Accompaniment Part (Cont'd.):

Coda